This workbook is cross-referenced to the revision guide, *OCR GCSE Additional Science A Revision Plus*, published by Lonsdale.

The questions and activities in this book will help to reinforce your understanding of the nine modules on the OCR GCSE Additional Science A specification (J631), from the Twenty First Century Science suite, providing excellent preparation for your exams.

You will have to sit four exams in total, including an Ideas in Context paper, which will test your ability to use and apply your scientific knowledge, for example, to understand and evaluate information about a current social-science issue. The questions on pages 87–90 of this workbook have been specially designed to allow you to practise these skills.

This workbook is suitable for use by Foundation and Higher Tier students.

HT Any material that is limited to Higher Tier students appears inside a grey tinted box, clearly labelled with the symbol **HT**.

A Note to Teachers

The pages in this workbook can be used as…

- classwork sheets – students can use the revision guide to answer the questions
- harder classwork sheets – pupils study the topic and then answer the questions without using the revision guide
- easy-to-mark homework sheets – to test pupils' understanding and reinforce their learning
- the basis for learning homework tasks which are then tested in subsequent lessons
- test material for topics or entire units
- a structured revision programme prior to the objective tests / written exams.

Answers to these worksheets are available to order.

The author and publisher would like to thank everyone who has contributed to this book:

IFC   ©iStockphoto.com / Andrei Tchernov

ISBN 9781905129706

Published by Lonsdale
An imprint of HarperCollins*Publishers*
77–85 Fulham Palace Road
London W6 8JB

© 2006, 2009 Lonsdale

Project Editor: Charlotte Christensen

Authors / Editors: Nathan Goodman, Tracey Cowell, Eliot Attridge

Cover and Concept Design: Sarah Duxbury

Design: Graeme Brown and Anne-Marie Taylor

All rights reserved. No part of this publication may be reproduced, stored in a retrieval system, or transmitted, in any form or by any means, electronic, mechanical, photocopying, recording or otherwise, without the prior permission of Lonsdale.

Printed in the UK

FSC is a non-profit international organisation established to promote the responsible management of the world's forests. Products carrying the FSC label are independently certified to assure consumers that they come from forests that are managed to meet the social, economic and ecological needs of present and future generations.

Find out more about HarperCollins and the environment at
www.harpercollins.co.uk/green

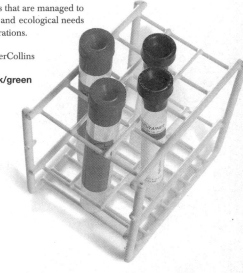

Contents

Contents

Unit 1
- 4 B4: Homeostasis
- 13 C4: Chemical Patterns
- 23 P4: Explaining Motion

Unit 2
- 33 B5: Growth and Development
- 40 C5: Chemicals of the Natural Environment
- 50 P5: Electric Circuits

Unit 3
- 58 B6: Brain and Mind
- 68 C6: Chemical Synthesis
- 79 P6: The Wave Model of Radiation

Unit 4
- 87 Ideas in Context

- 91 Glossary
- 96 Periodic Table

Homeostasis

1 a) Briefly explain what homeostasis is.

b) How is homeostasis achieved?

2 The human body has automatic control systems which ensure the correct, steady levels of two factors. What are the two factors?

a) _____ b) _____

3 What could be the consequence of failing to maintain homeostasis?

4 The table below shows how the body loses water.

a) An adult loses 3000cm³ of water in one day. Complete the table to show the volume of water lost through each method.

How Water is Lost	Percentage	Volume of Water Lost Every day
Urine	40	i)
Faeces	5	ii)
Sweat	45	iii)
Breathing	10	iv)

b) If vigorous exercise is taken in hot weather, what will the body do to maintain…

i) temperature? _____

ii) water content? _____

5 a) Athletes sweat more when they are exercising. Give two reasons why they sweat?

i) _____

ii) _____

b) What do athletes need to do to ensure homeostasis?

6 Name the medical condition that occurs once the body has lost too much heat to the environment.

Homeostasis

1 a) Some individuals are not able to maintain their own homeostasis. Give two examples of such individuals.

i) ....

ii) ....

b) For one of your answers in **a)** above, name the artificial system that would be used to maintain homeostasis.

....

2 Scuba divers need to maintain homeostasis whilst diving.

List three problems that will need to be overcome by a diver diving in the North Sea.

a) ....

b) ....

c) ....

3 What is the purpose of scuba diving equipment?

....

....

4 A mountaineer faces different challenges when climbing a mountain. Why is lack of oxygen a problem on the highest mountains?

....

....

5 Explain why it is important to drink more water in hot weather.

....

6 Explain, in as much detail as you can, what negative feedback is.

....

....

....

....

Homeostasis

1 Explain what is meant by the term **diffusion**.

....
....
....

2 Give an example of diffusion occurring in plants.

....
....
....

3 Explain what is meant by the term **osmosis**.

....
....
....

4 The diagram below shows an experiment to demonstrate osmosis. Explain what happened in the experiment, and why.

Thistle funnel
30 mins later
Pure water
Sugar solution
Visking tubing

....
....
....
....

5 Which of the following are examples of osmosis? Tick the correct box(es).

a) Water evaporating from leaves. ☐

b) Water moving from plant cell to plant cell. ☐

c) Mixing pure water and sugar solution. ☐

d) Ink spreading through water. ☐

e) A pear losing water in a concentrated salt solution. ☐

f) Water moving from blood to body cells. ☐

g) Sugar absorbed from the intestines into the blood. ☐

6 Nadia lives by the sea. Occasionally her garden is flooded by seawater and the plants in her garden wilt and die. Explain why flooding with sea water causes the plants to wilt.

....
....
....

Homeostasis

1 a) Animal cells have no cell wall. Why, therefore, can osmosis have a serious effect on the cell? Give two reasons.

  i) ....

  ....

  ii) ....

  ....

b) What do animals that live in freshwater need to do to prevent damage to their cells?

....

....

c) What do animals that live in saltwater need to do to prevent damage to their cells?

....

....

2 a) Explain what is meant by the term **active transport**.

....

....

b) Give an example of when a cell uses active transport.

....

....

3 a) What are enzymes?

....

b) What do enzymes do?

....

Homeostasis

4 Temperature affects the rate at which enzymes work. An experiment was carried out to investigate how temperature affects the rate at which an enzyme converts starch into sugar.

The results are shown in the table below. A black dot means starch is still present. A grey dot means no starch is present.

TEMPERATURE (°C)	TIME (min)						
	10	20	30	40	50	60	70
10	●	●	●	●	●	●	○
20	●	●	●	●	●	○	○
30	●	●	●	○	○	○	○
40	●	●	○	○	○	○	○
50	●	●	●	●	●	○	○
60	●	●	●	●	●	●	●

a) At what temperature does the enzyme work best?

b) Why do you think it works best at this temperature?

c) Why does the bottom row of the table contain only black dots?

d) Explain what has happened to the enzyme.

5 Explain what the 'lock and key' model is.

6 a) What two factors can denature an enzyme?

i) _____ ii) _____

b) If an enzyme becomes denatured, what happens to the active site?

Homeostasis

1 In humans, at what temperature do enzymes work best?

2 Name two locations of temperature detectors in the human body.

   a) ....

   b) ....

3 What is the function of the brain in maintaining a constant internal body temperature?

4 Name the effectors which carry out the response when controlling temperature.

   a) ....

   b) ....

5 Describe what happens when the temperature of the body increases too much, and the body needs to get rid of excess heat.

6 a) Megan is suffering from heat stroke. If she does not receive treatment, she may die. List four symptoms that Megan might have.

   i) ....

   ii) ....

   iii) ....

   iv) ....

   b) List two treatments of heat stroke.

   i) ....

   ii) ....

Homeostasis

1 Explain what the hypothalamus does.

2 a) What is meant by the term **vasodilation**?

b) Explain how vasodilation helps the body in hot conditions.

3 a) What is meant by the term **vasoconstriction**?

b) Explain how vasoconstriction helps the body in cold conditions.

4 Iqbal is a mountaineer. He is climbing with his friends when he falls from the rock surface. When his friends finally manage to get down to his position, they realise he is suffering from hypothermia.

a) Below what core body temperature will hypothermia occur?

b) List four symptoms that Iqbal might be showing.

i) _____ ii) _____

iii) _____ iv) _____

c) What should Iqbal's friends do to save his life? List three treatments.

i) _____

ii) _____

iii) _____

Homeostasis

1 It is the kidneys' job to control the balance of water in the body. How do they do this?

_____

2 Are the following statements **true** or **false**? If the sentence is false, underline the incorrect word that would need to be amended to make the sentence correct. The first one has been done for you.

a) The kidneys filter <u>large</u> molecules from the blood to form urine (water, salt and urea).   False

b) The kidneys absorb all the sugar for respiration.   _____

c) The kidneys excrete as much salt as the body requires.   _____

d) The kidneys absorb as much water as the body requires.   _____

e) The kidneys excrete the remaining urine, which is stored in the kidneys.   _____

3 a) Name two ways in which water can be lost from the body.

   i) _____   ii) _____

b) Name two ways in which the body can gain water.

   i) _____   ii) _____

4 List five factors that influence the amount of water that needs to be absorbed by the body.

a) _____

b) _____

c) _____

d) _____

e) _____

5 Alcohol and caffeine (found in coffee) are diuretics. What does the word **diuretic** mean?

_____

6 Taking drugs such as Ecstasy can cause water to build up in the blood. What is a consequence of this water build up?

_____

Homeostasis

1 What is the name of the hormone that controls the concentration of urine?

_____

2 Complete the missing labels in the diagram below, showing how urine concentration is controlled by the body.

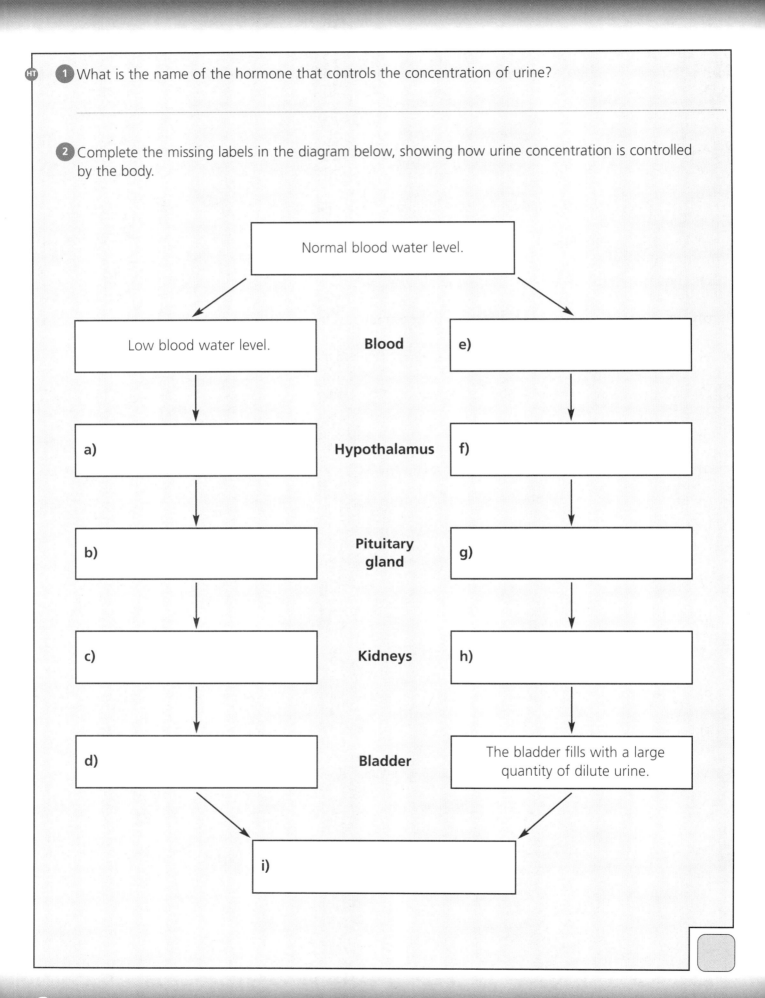

Chemical Patterns

1 Use the Periodic Table on p.96 to help you answer the following questions.

a) Roughly, how many elements are there in the Periodic Table? ....

b) i) What is a vertical column of elements known as?

....

ii) Name three elements in Group 2 of the Periodic Table.

....

iii) With the exception of helium, what is the connection between elements in the same group and the number of electrons in the outermost shell of an element?

....

....

iv) How many electrons are in the outermost shell of Group 4 elements?

....

c) i) What is a horizontal row of elements known as?

....

ii) Name three elements in the fourth period.

....

iii) What is the connection between the period to which the element belongs and the number of shells of electrons it has?

....

....

iv) How many shells of electrons do silver (Ag) and tin (Sn) have?

Silver: .... **Tin:** ....

d) i) What is the element symbol for hafnium? ....

ii) What is the mass number for hafnium? ....

iii) What is the atomic number for hafnium? ....

Chemical Patterns

1 a) Label the diagram to show the two main parts of an atom.

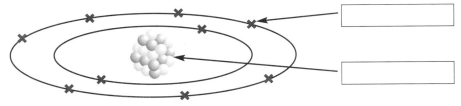

b) What is the relative charge of…

   i) a proton? _____

   ii) a neutron? _____

   iii) an electron? _____

   iv) an atom as a whole? _____

c) What is the relative mass of…

   i) a proton? _____

   ii) a neutron? _____

   iii) an electron? _____

2 a) A piece of nichrome wire is dipped into compounds of the following elements and then put into a Bunsen flame. What colour is the flame in each case?

   i) Lithium: _____

   ii) Sodium: _____

   iii) Potassium: _____

b) In each case, the light emitted from the flame produces a characteristic line spectrum. What does each line in the spectrum represent?

_____

_____

c) Why is the study of spectra so important?

_____

Chemical Patterns

1 a) Briefly explain what electron configuration means.

b) The electron configuration of potassium is 2.8.8.1. What does this tell us about…

  i) the maximum number of electrons that are in each shell?

  ii) the group that potassium belongs to in the Periodic Table?

  iii) the period that potassium belongs to in the Periodic Table?

2 Using the information provided below, write down the electron configuration for the following elements:

a) Calcium
Atomic No. = 20
No. of electrons = 20

b) Lithium
Atomic No. = 3
No. of electrons = 3

c) Boron
Atomic No. = 5
No. of electrons = 5

d) Chlorine
Atomic No. = 17
No. of electrons = 17

Chemical Patterns

1 Explain, in terms of atoms, why the total mass of the products of a chemical reaction is always equal to the total mass of the reactants.

_____

_____

2 a) Write down the word equation for the reaction shown in the table below.

Reactants			→	Products		
_____	+	_____	→	_____	+	_____
$NO_{(g)}$	+	$CO_{(g)}$	→	$N_{2(g)}$	+	$CO_{2(g)}$

b) The balanced symbol equation for this reaction is: $2NO_{(g)} + 2CO_{(g)} \longrightarrow N_{2(g)} + 2CO_{2(g)}$

In terms of molecules, what does this tell us?

_____

_____

3 a) Write a formula equation for the reaction between copper and oxygen to produce copper oxide.

[_____] + [_____] → [_____]

b) Explain, using diagrams to help you, how you would balance the equation.

_____

_____

c) Write down the balanced symbol equation for this chemical reaction.

_____

Chemical Patterns

1 What do each of the following hazard symbols mean? In each case, briefly explain what impact the substances can have.

a) ....

b) ....

c) ....

2 a) List one safety precaution you would need to take if a material had a 'highly flammable' symbol.

....

b) List two safety precautions you would need to take if a material had an 'irritant' symbol.

i) ....

ii) ....

3 a) How many metals are there in Group 1 of the Periodic Table? ....

b) As you go down the Group, what happens to the **i)** boiling points **ii)** reactivity, and **iii)** density?

i) .... ii) .... iii) ....

c) Complete the table below to show what happens, and what is produced, when alkali metals react with oxygen, water and chlorine.

Alkali Metals	Reaction with Oxygen	Reaction with Water	Reaction with Chlorine
Lithium, Li	Alkali metals are stored under oil because they react very vigorously with oxygen and water.	i)	ii)
Sodium, Na	They quickly tarnish in moist air, go dull and become covered in a layer of metal oxide.	Floats and melts – aggressive reaction. Metal hydroxide and hydrogen gas are formed.	iii)
Potassium, K	iv)	v)	vi)

Chemical Patterns

4 a) Write word equations for...

   i) the reaction of potassium with chlorine

   ii) the reaction of lithium with water

   iii) the reaction of sodium with oxygen.

b) For each of the reactions above, write the formula for the alkali metal compound formed. The first one has been done for you.

   i) KCL

   ii)

   iii)

HT

5 Write general equations, using M to refer to the alkali metal, for...

   a) the reaction with oxygen

   b) the reaction with water.

---

6 a) If you were checking the pH level of the solution formed when sodium is added to water, what safety precautions should you take?

   i)

   ii)

   iii)

b) Once you had taken the necessary safety precautions, briefly explain what you would do and what you would see during this process.

Chemical Patterns

1 a) How many non-metals are there in Group 7 of the Periodic Table?

_____

b) As you go down the Group, what happens to the **i)** boiling points **ii)** reactivity, and **iii)** density?

i) _____ ii) _____ iii) _____

2 a) All halogens consist of diatomic molecules. What is a diatomic molecule?

_____

b) Write down two examples of diatomic molecules.

i) _____

ii) _____

3 Complete the table below to show what the halogens look like, what they are used for, and the compounds formed when they react with sodium and metal hydroxides.

Halogen	Appearance at Room Temperature / Pressure	Uses	Compound Formed When Reacting with:	
			Hydroxide	Alkali Metal (Sodium)
Chlorine, Cl	Green gas	a)	b)	c)
Bromine, Br	d)	Bromine can be used to bleach dyes and kill bacteria in water.	e)	f)
Iodine, I	g)	h)	HI	i)

4 What kind of reaction is the following word equation an example of?

Potassium bromide + Chlorine ⟶ Potassium chloride + Bromine

_____

Chemical Patterns

1 a) Briefly explain, in terms of numbers of electrons, why all the alkali metals and all the halogens have similar properties.

b) Why do alkali metals become more reactive as you go down the group?

c) Why do halogens become less reactive as you go down the group?

2 a) Briefly explain what would happen in an experiment which showed that molten compounds, such as lithium chloride, conduct electricity.

b) What is another name for the charged particles in molten compounds?

3 a) Briefly explain your understanding of the term **ion**, in terms of electrons.

b) What is the difference between a cation and an anion?

Chemical Patterns

1 Which group of compounds of metals and elements in the Periodic Table are ionic compounds?

2 Using the diagrams below, explain, in terms of electrons, how potassium and chlorine bond ionically to form potassium chloride (KCl).

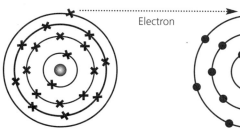
K Atom 2.8.8.1

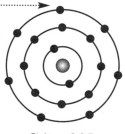
Cl Atom 2.8.7

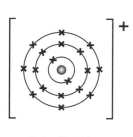
K^+ Ion $[2.8.8]^+$

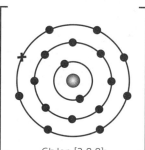
Cl^- Ion $[2.8.8]^-$

3 I am formed when positive ions and negative ions are electrostatically attracted to each other. What am I?

4 Potassium (K) and oxygen (O_2) bond ionically to form potassium oxide, K_2O. Each potassium atom has 1 electron in its outer shell. An oxygen atom wants 2 electrons, so 2 potassium atoms are needed. The atoms have become K^+, K^+ and O^{2-}, and the compound formed is potassium oxide, K_2O.

Using the information provided above, draw diagrams to illustrate how potassium and oxygen bond ionically.

Chemical Patterns

5 Using the diagrams below, explain, in terms of electrons, how calcium and oxygen bond ionically to form calcium oxide (CaO).

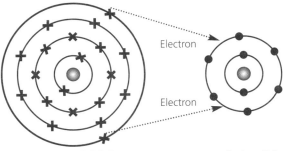
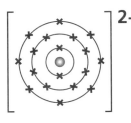
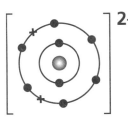

Ca atom 2.8.8.2   O atom 2.6 Ca^{2+} ion $[2.8.8]^{2+}$ O^{2-} ion $[2.8]^{2-}$

6 Explain, in terms of ions, why ionic compounds have high melting and boiling points, and conduct electricity when they are in solution or molten, but not when they are solid.

7 a) Write down the formulae for the following ionic compounds, using the information provided about the charge given on both ions.

    i) Lithium hydroxide   1+ + 1−   Formula = _____

    ii) Lithium oxide   1+ + 2−   Formula = _____

    iii) Aluminium oxide   3+ + 2−   Formula = _____

b) Write down the charge on the first ion, using the formula provided and the information about the charge for the other ion.

    i) $Mg(OH)_2$. $(OH)_2$ = 2 × 1− = 2−   Charge on first ion = _____

    ii) CuO. O = 2−   Charge on first ion = _____

    iii) $Fe_2(SO_4)_3$. $(SO_4)_3$ = 3 × 2− = 6−   Charge on first ion = _____

Explaining Motion

1) What is the difference between speed and velocity?

2) If a car has a velocity of +10m/s, what is its velocity when it is travelling in the opposite direction at the same speed?

3) A man walks +10 metres and then -5 metres. What is…

a) the total distance travelled?

b) the man's distance from the start point?

4) Write down the formula for calculating speed.

5) Complete the following table:

Speed (m/s)	Distance (m)	Time (s)
15	45	v)
6	60	vi)
i)	100	10
ii)	300	60
25	iii)	4
30	iv)	20

6) What is the difference between average speed and instantaneous speed?

Explaining Motion

7) A child playing in the playground runs at 4m/s for 3 seconds, stops for 5 seconds and then runs at 4m/s for 2 seconds. Calculate...

a) the distance travelled in the first 3 seconds ....

b) the distance travelled in the next 5 seconds ....

c) the distance travelled in the last 2 seconds ....

d) the total distance travelled ....

e) the total time taken ....

f) the average speed. ....

8) A car travels 15 miles from Sheffield to Doncaster in a time of 30 minutes. The car stops in Doncaster for 1 hour, and then returns to Sheffield, again taking 30 minutes to travel the 15 miles.

a) How fast is the car travelling from Sheffield to Doncaster?

....

b) What is the average speed for the entire 2 hours?

....

9) Sketch the following distance–time graphs.

a) A woman remaining stationary 5m from a starting point (0).

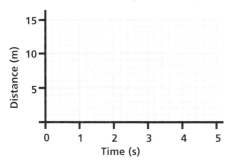

b) A runner travelling at a constant speed of 5m/s.

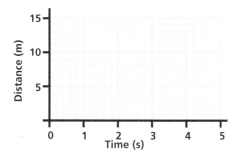

Explaining Motion

1) The graph below shows a car's journey.

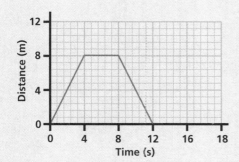

a) What is the average velocity of this journey? ....

b) What is the average speed of this journey? ....

2) On a distance–time graph what does a curved line indicate?

....

3) Sketch a distance–time graph showing a jogger starting from rest and running 7m in 5 seconds at an increasing speed.

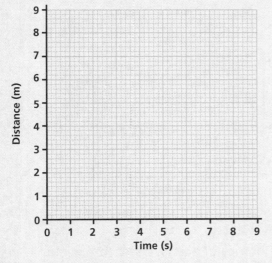

4) Sketch a distance–time graph of a cyclist travelling at 4m/s for 2 seconds and then gradually slowing down to come to rest 6m from the start position in 4 seconds.

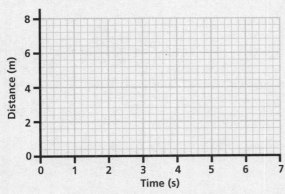

Explaining Motion

1) What does the slope of a velocity–time graph represent?

_____

2) On the graphs below, sketch the following velocity–time graphs, illustrating…

   a) an object at rest

   b) an object travelling at a constant velocity of 5m/s

   c) an object accelerating at a constant rate of 5m/s^2

   d) an object decelerating at a constant rate from 5m/s^2 to rest.

a)
b)

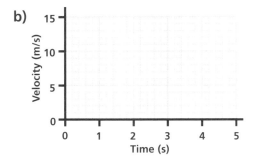

c)

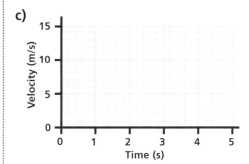

d)

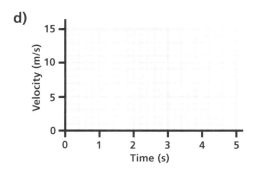

3) Velocity–time graphs are used as tachographs to record the journey of a lorry. Describe the journey depicted by the tachograph below.

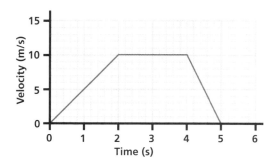

_____

_____

_____

_____

Explaining Motion

1) How does a force occur?

....

2) Complete the table below to give the names and descriptions of four forces.

Name of Force	Description of Force
a)	Acts to slow things down when two surfaces rub against each other.
Air Resistance	b) ....
c)	Pushes up on the bottom of a cup sitting on a table and stops the cup sinking into the table.
Gravity	d) ....

3) Whenever something exerts a force it experiences an equal and opposite force. Explain how this principle is used in jet engines.

....

....

....

4) What is the resultant force?

....

5) The following diagrams illustrate a car travelling at 30mph. Calculate the resultant force and state what happens to the motion of the car.

a)  1000N ← 🚗 → 4000N

b)  2000N ← 🚗 → 0N

c) 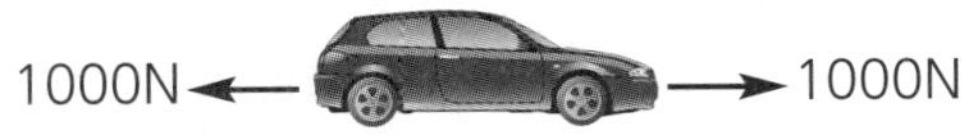 1000N ← 🚗 → 1000N

Explaining Motion

6 How do forces such as friction and reaction occur?

_____

7 Explain the forces at work when an object is resting on a surface.

_____

8 A car parked on a hill experiences a force of 5000N from gravity trying to pull it down the hill. Which of the following is the value of friction?

a) Zero ☐   b) Less than 5000N ☐

c) 5000N ☐   d) More than 5000N ☐

9 The friction on a car travelling at a constant speed is 400N and the air resistance is 300N. Which of the following is the correct value for the force from the engine?

a) Zero ☐   b) 300N ☐   c) 400N ☐

d) 700N ☐   e) More than 700N ☐

10 A car with a weight of 10 000N is parked on a horizontal surface. What is the force of friction caused by the brakes?

a) Zero ☐   b) Less than 10 000N ☐

c) 10 000N ☐ d) More than 10 000N ☐

11 A car with a weight of 10 000N is parked on a horizontal surface. What is the value of the reaction force?

a) Zero ☐   b) Less than 10 000N ☐

c) 10 000N ☐ d) More than 10 000N ☐

12 A car with a weight of 10 000N is travelling at a constant speed on a horizontal surface. What is the value of the reaction force?

a) Zero ☐   b) Less than 10 000N ☐

c) 10 000N ☐ d) More than 10 000N ☐

Explaining Motion

1) Which two physical properties does momentum depend on?

a) .... b) ....

2) Complete the following table.

Momentum (kg m/s)	Mass (kg)	Velocity (m/s)
a)	50	10
b)	1000	30
3000	c)	30
800	d)	2
100	e)	50
20 000	f)	20

3) When a force causes a change in momentum what two things does the size of the change in momentum depend on?

a) .... b) ....

4) a) A car travelling at 30m/s has a mass of 1000kg. What is its momentum?

b) The car applies its brakes for 5 seconds. The brakes exert a constant force of 2000N. Assuming no other forces are involved, what is the change of momentum?

c) What is the new momentum of the car?

d) What is the new velocity of the car?

5) A motorcycle with a mass of 500kg is travelling at 20m/s. If the rider applies the brakes for 2 seconds, and the brakes exert a constant force of 5000N, what is the new momentum of the motorcycle?

6) A car of mass 1500kg has a momentum of 22 500kg m/s. What is its velocity?

Explaining Motion

1 During a collision the occupants of a vehicle undergo a change in momentum and experience the force of the collision. Using the idea of momentum…

a) explain why the occupants of the car are more likely to suffer serious injuries when the vehicle is travelling faster

b) explain why the occupants of the car are more likely to suffer serious injuries if the collision takes place over a shorter period of time.

2 Crumple zones are a very important car-safety feature. How does a crumple zone reduce the injuries sustained by the occupants of the vehicle?

3 A car travelling at 30m/s is involved in an accident and comes to a halt in 0.1 seconds. A passenger in the car has a mass of 50kg. Calculate…

a) the momentum of the passenger before the accident

b) the momentum of the passenger after the accident

c) the change in momentum of the passenger

d) the force acting on the passenger during the accident.

Explaining Motion

4 Are the following statements **true** or **false**?

a) An object has more kinetic energy if it has a greater mass. _____

b) An object has more kinetic energy if it is travelling faster. _____

c) An object travelling in space has no kinetic energy. _____

d) Doubling the mass of an object doubles its kinetic energy. _____

e) Doubling the speed of an object doubles its kinetic energy. _____

5 A moving object has kinetic energy. When a moving object comes to a halt, what has happened to its kinetic energy?

_____

_____

6 A man of 70kg is running at 5m/s. Calculate his kinetic energy.

_____

7 a) What is gravitational potential energy?

_____

_____

b) How much energy is needed to lift a 100N weight to a height of 5m?

_____

_____

c) What happens to an object's gravitational potential energy when it falls?

_____

HT 8 A 1kg book falls 1m off a table. How much kinetic energy does it have when it hits the floor?

_____

9 Complete the following sentence:

When work is being done _____ is being transferred. When work is done by an object it _____ energy and when work is done on an object it _____ energy.

Explaining Motion

10) How much work is done by a crane when it raises a 1200kg car to a height of 5m?

11) The engine of a train travelling at a constant speed provides a constant driving force of 50 000N in order to overcome resistive forces.

How much work is done by the engine in travelling a distance of 20km?

12) A 50kg skydiver jumps out of an airplane from a height of 2000m.

   a) By the time she reaches the ground how much work has been done on her by gravity?

   b) If all of the work done was used to increase her kinetic energy, how much kinetic energy would she have when she reached the ground?

   c) Reaching the ground with such a large amount of kinetic energy would be fatal. In reality she reaches the ground with much less kinetic energy. Most of the work done by gravity is used up in overcoming another force.

   What is the name of this force?

   d) With what speed would she reach the ground?

Growth and Development

1 a) What does DNA determine?

b) What is the correct name given to the shape that DNA molecules form? Tick the correct answer.

  i) Single helix ☐   **ii)** Spiral ☐   **iii)** Crystal ☐   **iv)** Double helix ☐

2 Write the correct word alongside each definition.

  a) The wall of a plant cell is made of this.

  b) Most cells have one of these; it contains genetic information.

  c) All cells have one of these; it controls the movement of substances into and out of the cell.

  d) This is where protein synthesis occurs.

  e) This is found only in plant cells and is filled with sap.

3 What is the definition of **mitosis**?

4 What two things happen during the growth cycle of a cell?

  a)

  b)

5 Why are the organelles and chromosomes copied before the cell divides into daughter cells?

6 For the following statements write **mitosis** and / or **meiosis**, as appropriate, by the side of each one.

  a) Cell division.

  b) Involved in asexual reproduction.

  c) Produces cells with the same number of chromosomes.

  d) Involved in sexual reproduction.

  e) Produces genetically identical clones.

Growth and Development

1 What is the definition of **fertilisation**?

2 What is the name given to a fertilised cell?

3 Why must meiosis occur before fertilisation?

4 Complete the following statement about fertilisation:

One .... in each pair comes from the .... and the other comes from the .... This is why it is important that the .... produced during .... only has half the number of .... as the parent ....

5 When the zygote divides it forms an embryo. What will the embryonic cells develop into?

6 Approximately how many cells make up an average human?

7 Why do meiosis and sexual reproduction produce variation?

8 In the space below draw a diagram to show the process of fertilisation and the development of a new embryo.

Growth and Development

1 Growth and development in organisms are governed by genes present on chromosomes in each cell nucleus. How do the genes determine characteristics such as the ability to be able to roll your tongue?

....

....

2 The instructions are in the form of a code made up of four bases which hold the molecule together.

   a) What are the names of the bases?

   i) ....

   ii) ....

   iii) ....

   iv) ....

   b) The bases always pair up in the same way. Which bases pair up together?

   i) ....

   ii) ....

   c) Draw a diagram to show how the bases pair together.

3 Chromosomes always stay inside the nucleus. How does the genetic code leave the cell to get to the cytoplasm?

....

....

....

HT

4 How many amino acids can be formed from the possible pool of three base pairs?

....

5 What is the structure of a protein dependent upon?

....

Growth and Development

1) By what process does a zygote divide to form an embryo?

2) At what stage do embryo cells start to develop into specialised cells?

3) Give two differences between genetically identical cells in a developing embryo at the 16-cell stage.

   a)

   b)

4) Which genes are active in any given cell?

5) Roughly how many genes are there in human DNA?

HT 6) Name the three locations that stem cells can be collected from.

   a)

   b)

   c)

7) What is therapeutic cloning?

8) a) What is the problem with using adult stem cells?

   b) What is the advantage with using adult stem cells?

Growth and Development

1 Plant cells, like animal cells, divide by the process of mitosis. What is the difference in the rate of growth between plant and animal cells?

....

....

2 a) What is a meristem?

....

....

b) What is so special about the cells from a meristem?

....

c) What areas of growth are **i)** apical, and **ii)** lateral meristems concerned with?

  i) ....

  ii) ....

d) Sketch a cross-section of a stem, labelling where the lateral meristems are located.

3 a) Explain what a callus is.

....

....

b) How can a callus be created?

....

....

c) How can a callus be induced to grow into specialised plant tissue?

....

Growth and Development

1 Briefly explain what the xylem tubes are used for.

2 Briefly explain what the phloem tubes are used for.

3 Explain the processes by which a cloned plant is produced.

4 a) Why does a plant need to respond to light?

   b) What is this response called?

5 Some watercress seedlings are put into a cardboard box which has a hole cut out at the side. A light source is directed through the hole.

Sketch a diagram showing what would happen to the direction of growth of the seedlings.

6 a) What is the name given to the main group of plant hormones used in agriculture?

   b) Whereabouts in plants are these hormones produced?

Growth and Development

7 Explain, with the help of the diagram, what auxins do to cells that are furthest away from a light source.

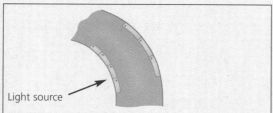

8 For each of the experiments below, explain what will happen to the plant shoot.

a)
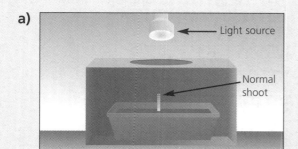

b)
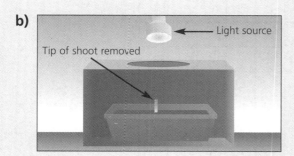

c)
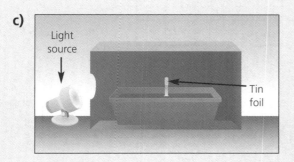

d)
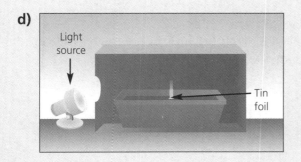

Chemicals of the Natural Environment

1 Find the answers to the following clues in the wordsearch below. The definitions all relate to the structure of the Earth.

a) 9 letters   All living organisms on the Earth, including plants, animals and microorganisms.

b) 10 letters   A layer of gas surrounding the Earth.

c) 11 letters   i) All the water on the Earth, including oceans, rivers, lakes, and underground reserves. The water contains dissolved compounds.

   ii) The rigid outer layer of the Earth made up of the crust and the part of the mantle just below it.

I	A	B	L	E	S	U	T	F	O	W	T	M
C	W	G	X	C	S	L	G	A	N	H	N	E
O	A	S	A	M	E	A	V	G	Y	T	M	L
M	T	V	O	B	R	E	W	D	R	E	P	E
P	M	T	Y	I	T	T	R	S	O	R	E	V
O	O	I	L	O	I	O	T	L	D	F	C	V
U	S	H	U	S	S	N	C	A	X	C	V	P
N	P	B	K	P	E	D	P	C	Z	B	N	Y
D	H	F	H	H	U	R	N	I	Q	W	L	O
S	E	E	E	E	D	F	R	M	C	X	Z	A
R	R	F	Y	R	P	G	S	E	T	Y	E	C
E	E	R	Y	E	G	A	S	H	R	J	K	L
I	L	I	T	H	O	S	P	H	E	R	E	S
P	R	O	P	E	R	T	I	E	S	T	W	Y

2 Name three elements that are abundant in the rigid outer layer of the Earth (see your answer to question **1 c) ii)**.

a) _____   b) _____

c) _____

3 All living organisms on the Earth, including plants, animals and microorganisms, are made up from compounds containing elements. Name the four main elements.

a) _____   b) _____

c) _____   d) _____

Chemicals of the Natural Environment

1 Name two main chemicals that have their own life cycles.

a) .... b) ....

2 Briefly explain what you understand by the term **carbon cycle**.

....

....

....

....

3 Use the flow chart of the nitrogen cycle to answer the following questions.

The Nitrogen Cycle

a) Which sphere does N_2 in the atmosphere move into?

....

b) What happens when plants and animals (biosphere) die?

....

c) How do nitrates in the soil (NO_3) return to the atmosphere?

....

4 Name one human activity that may upset the balance of the natural cycles.

....

Chemicals of the Natural Environment

1 Name the five main chemicals that make up the atmosphere.

a) ....

b) ....

c) ....

d) ....

e) ....

2 a) What do the low boiling and melting points of four of the molecules making up the atmosphere tell us about them?

....

b) Using the information in part **a)**, briefly describe the structure of the molecules in the atmosphere.

....

....

....

c) What is the electrical charge of these molecules?

....

d) i) How are the atoms within these molecules connected?

....

ii) Why are these 'connections' in place? Draw a diagram to help explain your answer.

....

....

....

Chemicals of the Natural Environment

1) Why is seawater salty?

2) Name three salts that are found in seawater.

a) .... b) ....

c) ....

3) Why is it unusual that a small molecule like water has a boiling point of 100°C?

4) Briefly describe the structure and properties of a polar water molecule.

5) What helps water to dissolve ionic compounds?

6) Silicon, oxygen and aluminium are the three most abundant elements in the Earth's crust.

a) Which compound is produced from two of these elements?

b) What are the four key properties of this compound?

i) ....

ii) ....

iii) ....

iv) ....

Chemicals of the Natural Environment

7 List two materials in which silicon dioxide is present.

a) .... b) ....

8 Explain, in terms of covalent structure, why…

a) silica glass, which is an electrical insulator, might be used as an insulator in electrical devices.

....

b) silicon dioxide, which has a very high melting point, might be used to make furnace linings.

....

9 Name the three important groups of molecules that make up a large part of the biosphere.

a) ....

b) ....

c) ....

10 Glucose is a carbohydrate. How do we know this?

....

11 The table below shows the approximate percentage composition of the elements in a protein, two fats and DNA.

	% Carbon	% Hydrogen	% Oxygen	% Nitrogen	% Phosphorus
Protein	30	5	40	25	0
Fat 1	40	10	50	0	0
Fat 2	38	12	50	0	0
DNA	40	5	30	22	3

Use the table to answer the following questions:

a) Which fat contains the higher percentage of hydrogen? ....

b) Which is the only molecule to contain any phosphorus? ....

c) Which molecule contains the highest percentage of nitrogen? ....

Chemicals of the Natural Environment

1 a) How do we know if an equation is balanced?

....

....

b) If an equation needs to be balanced, what two key things do you need to remember?

  i) ....

  ....

  ii) ....

  ....

2 a) Write down the symbol equation for the reaction below.

Copper + Oxygen ⟶ Copper oxide

b) Briefly explain why this equation is not balanced.

....

c) Write down the balanced symbol equation for this chemical reaction.

....

3 a) Briefly describe what you understand by the term **relative atomic mass**.

....

....

b) What is the symbol for relative atomic mass?

....

c) i) Which of the two numbers given for each element in the Periodic Table is the relative atomic mass?

....

  ii) What else does this number represent?

  ....

Chemicals of the Natural Environment

1 a) What is the name used to describe the naturally occurring elements and compounds in the lithosphere? _____

b) What is an ore? _____

2 The method of extracting metals from ores depends on a metal's position in the reactivity series.

a) Why are sodium, calcium, magnesium and aluminium particularly difficult to extract? _____

b) What is one of the main methods used to extract these metals? _____

c) i) Zinc, iron and lead are below a key metal in the reactivity series. Which metal is this? _____

ii) How are zinc, iron and lead extracted from their ores? _____

d) Name two metals that exist naturally and can be extracted using physical processes such as panning.

i) _____ ii) _____

HT 3 a) Find the mass of Cu that can be extracted from 100g of CuO.

_____

b) Calculate this mass again using the equation below to find the ratio of the Cu (product) that can be made from 100g of CuO (reactant).

$$2CuO + C \longrightarrow 2Cu + CO_2$$

_____

Chemicals of the Natural Environment

1 a) What kind of analysis do you need to carry out in order to assess the impact on the environment of extracting and using metals?

....

b) What are the three main stages of this analysis?

i) .... ii) .... iii) ....

2 a) What are the two main environmental factors which impact on the manufacture and use of products?

i) ....

ii) ....

b) Which three processes relate to the disposal stage of this type of analysis?

i) .... ii) .... iii) ....

3 a) Briefly describe what you understand by the term **electrolysis**.

....

b) Where is this process used?

....

4 What needs to happen to an ionic compound before it will conduct electricity?

....

....

5 When a direct electric current is passed through a liquid containing positive and negative ions that are free to move throughout the liquid, (e.g. molten lead bromide), what happens?

....

....

HT

6 a) What is the term used to describe what happens when the ions get to the oppositely charged electrode?

....

b) What does this term mean? ....

Chemicals of the Natural Environment

1 a) Why does aluminium need to be obtained from its ore by electrolysis?

b) For the electrolysis of aluminium to take place, what must the solution of the cell contain?

c) What happens to the mixture to allow the ions to move freely?

d) i) When a current is passed through the mixture, what happens at the negative electrode (cathode)?

ii) What happens at the positive electrode (anode)?

e) Why is the extraction of aluminium by this method expensive?

f) Write a formula equation for this reaction.

g) Write a half-equation to show what happens at the negative electrode during electrolysis.

h) Write a half-equation to show what happens at the positive electrode during electrolysis.

Chemicals of the Natural Environment

1 a) Generally speaking, which four properties are associated with metals?

   i) ....

   ii) ....

   iii) ....

   iv) ....

b) Explain, in terms of structure and metallic bonds, why a metal might have each of these properties.

   i) ....

   ii) ....

   iii) ....

   iv) ....

c) Complete the table below showing the properties and uses of different metals.

Metal	Property	Use
Copper	• Conducts electricity i) Conducts	• Cables • Electromagnets ii) ....
iii)	iv) .... • Strong	• Saucepans • Cars
v)	vi) .... vii) .... • Resistant to corrosion	• Drink cans • Windows
Titanium	• Very strong viii)	• Replacement hip joints ix) .... x) ....

ADDITIONAL SCIENCE WORKBOOK - Revision Guide Reference: Page 48

Electric Circuits

1 Complete the following sentences from the words below.

Static electricity occurs when _____ _____ builds up on an object. This can occur when _____ materials are rubbed against each other.

Electrons carry a _____ charge, therefore, if an object gains electrons it becomes _____ charged. For an object to become _____ charged it must _____ _____ .

| **positively** | **negative** | **lose** | **charge** | **insulating** |

| **electrons** | **negatively** | **electrical** |

2 For each of the following questions, tick the correct answer.

a) If both rods A and B are uncharged…
   i) nothing will happen ☐   ii) they will repel each other ☐   iii) they will attract each other ☐

b) If rod A is positively charged and rod B is negatively charged…
   i) nothing will happen ☐   ii) they will repel each other ☐   iii) they will attract each other ☐

c) If both rods A and B are positively charged…
   i) nothing will happen ☐   ii) they will repel each other ☐   iii) they will attract each other ☐

d) If both rods A and B are negatively charged…
   i) nothing will happen ☐   ii) they will repel each other ☐   iii) they will attract each other ☐

e) If rod A is uncharged and rod B is positively charged…
   i) nothing will happen ☐   ii) they will repel each other ☐   iii) they will attract each other ☐

3 A car is being spray-painted. Explain how the paint is evenly spread on the car.

_____

_____

_____

Electric Circuits

1 a) Briefly explain what an electric current is.

....

b) In what unit is current measured?

....

2 Explain why metals are good conductors of electric current.

....

....

....

3 Complete the table below.

Name	Symbol	Description
Cell	a)	Provides energy to 'push' the current around the circuit.
b)	c)	A group of cells acting together.
Filament lamp	d)	e)
f)	Ⓐ	g)
h)	Ⓥ	i)
Switch (closed)	j)	k)
l)	m)	A component whose resistance cannot be altered.

4 Explain the difference between alternating current and direct current.

....

....

....

5 What does the amount of current flowing through a circuit depend on?

....

....

6 What is potential difference? ....

....

7 How does the potential difference affect the amount of current that flows through a component?

....

....

Electric Circuits

1) What do we mean by the resistance of a component?

2) What effect does adding resistors have on the total resistance when they are added **a)** in series, and **b)** in parallel?

a)

b)

3) Explain how an electric current can cause a wire to melt.

4) Complete the table below.

Potential Difference (V)	Current (A)	Resistance (Ω)
20	2	a)
12	3	b)
32	1.5	c)
15	6	d)
8	3	e)

5) Complete the table below.

Potential Difference (V)	Current (A)	Resistance (Ω)
a)	1.5	100
b)	6	6
8	c)	20
16	d)	52

Electric Circuits

1 Sketch a graph showing the relationship between current and potential difference for a resistor at a constant temperature.

2 Complete the following sentences.

Some components have a resistance that will change depending on the environmental conditions. A _____ dependent resistor has a resistance that _____ when the light intensity increases. The symbol for an LDR is _____. A thermistor has a resistance that _____ when temperature _____.

HT

3 What happens to **a)** the total potential difference, and **b)** the current, when batteries are added in parallel?

a) _____

b) _____

4 What is the difference between a series circuit and a parallel circuit?

_____

_____

5 Sketch a diagram of **a)** a series circuit, and **b)** a parallel circuit, which has 1 battery and 2 bulbs.

a)

b)

6 A circuit has 1 battery and 2 resistors in parallel. Resistor A has a resistance of 2 ohms and resistor B has a resistance of 1 ohm. If the battery has a 3 amp current flowing through it, what is the current flowing through resistors A and B?

Resistor A: _____   Resistor B: _____

Electric Circuits

7 In a parallel circuit why do components with a lower resistance have a larger current running through them?

....
....
....

8 For the following diagrams, complete the readings on the ammeters and voltmeters.

a)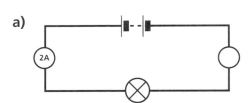

b)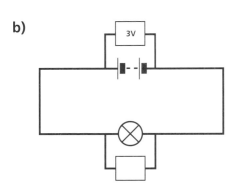

c)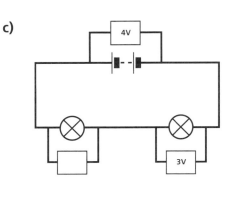

d)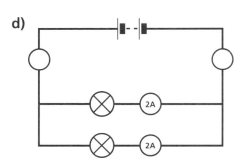

e)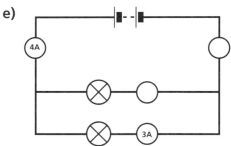

9 In a series circuit with two resistors, why does the one with the larger resistance end up with a greater share of the potential difference supplied by the battery?

....
....

Electric Circuits

1 Moving a magnet into a coil of wire can induce an electric current in the wire. Give two ways in which the direction of the current could be reversed.

a) ....

b) ....

2 a) How much current would flow if the magnet is held stationary inside the coil of wire?

....

b) Explain your answer to part **a)**.

....

3 An electric generator uses a rotating magnet inside a coil of wire. Suggest a reason why generators do not use a rotating coil and a fixed wire.

....

4 Suggest three ways of increasing the size of the induced voltage.

a) ....

b) ....

c) ....

5 a) Describe how the induced voltage across a coil changes during each revolution.

....

b) What kind of current is produced? ....

Electric Circuits

1) Power is the rate of energy transfer. What does this mean?

_____

_____

2) a) What is the formula for calculating power?

_____

b) When connected to a mains supply of 220 volts, an electric iron has a 10 amp current flowing through it. Calculate the power of the iron.

_____

c) If the same iron is connected to a supply of 110 volts, the iron has a 5 amp current flowing through it. How much power does the iron use now?

_____

HT

3) A 3kW heater is connected to a supply of 220 volts. Calculate the current.

_____

4) What are transformers used for? _____

_____

HT

5) a) A step-down transformer for mobile phones converts the 240 volts mains supply to 12 volts. If the primary coil has 2000 turns, how many turns are there on the secondary coil?

_____

_____

b) A transformer has 40 turns on the primary coil and 200 turns on the secondary coil. If the input voltage on the primary coil is 20 volts, what is the output voltage?

_____

_____

c) A step-up transformer in the National Grid converts 11 000 volts to 220 0000 volts. What is the ratio of primary turns to secondary turns?

_____

Electric Circuits

1 For the following questions, put a tick in the box by the correct answer.

  a) What is the scientific unit used for energy?

  i) Watt ☐   ii) Joule ☐   iii) Volt ☐   iv) Ampere ☐

  b) Which unit do we use for energy used in the home?

  i) Kilowatt hour ☐   ii) Kilowatt ☐   iii) Joule ☐   iv) Kilo joule ☐

  c) What is the correct formula for calculating energy?

  i) $E = \frac{p}{t}$ ☐   ii) $E = \frac{t}{p}$ ☐   iii) $E = p \times t$ ☐   iv) $E = I \times V$ ☐

2 A 60W light bulb is switched on for 1 minute. How much energy is used? (You must include the correct units in your answer.)

3 A 3kW heater is switched on for 30 minutes. How much energy is used? (You must include the correct units in your answer.)

4 If the energy cost is 5p per kWh, how much is the cost per day (24hrs) to run a household if the average power consumption is 2.5kW?

5 Complete the table below.

Electrical Appliance	Energy In (J)	Useful Energy Out (J)	Efficiency %
Tumble dryer	3000	2400 (heat and kinetic)	a)
Light bulb	60	6 (light)	b)
Electric motor	400	c)	50%

Brain and Mind

1 Fill in the missing words to complete the passage below, which describes what happens when organisms respond to stimuli.

Animals respond to _____ in order to keep themselves in _____ that will ensure their _____.

These _____ are co-ordinated by the _____ _____ _____.

2 The following all form the nervous system. Number them 1–7 to show the pathway for receiving information.

a) Spinal cord ☐   b) Effector ☐   c) Receptor ☐

d) Brain ☐   e) Relay neurons ☐

f) Sensory neurons ☐   g) Motor neurons ☐

3 a) In mammals, what is the function of the central nervous system?

b) In mammals, what is the function of the peripheral nervous system?

4 What is the difference between a motor neuron and a sensory neuron in terms of carrying electrical impulses? Draw diagrams to help explain your answer.

5 Explain what a receptor is.

Brain and Mind

6 Explain what an effector is.

_____

_____

7 There are receptors all over the human body. For each location given below, name one type of stimulus that is detected by the receptors found there. The first one has been completed for you.

a) Eyes   **Light**

b) Nose   _____

c) Ears   _____

d) Skin   _____

e) Tongue _____

8 The specialised cells that make up muscle tissue are effectors.

Describe in two steps how muscles contract.

Step 1: _____

_____

Step 2: _____

_____

9 Describe the path that light travels when it enters the eye.

_____

_____

_____

10 Describe what happens when a signal is sent by the nervous system to hormone-secreting cells in a gland.

_____

_____

_____

Brain and Mind

1 a) What are neurons?

b) Why are neurons elongated?

c) Why do neurons have branched endings?

2 What is an axon?

3 What is the function of the fatty sheath that surrounds many neurons?

4 a) What is a synapse?

b) Approximately how many synapses does the average adult human brain have? ....

c) Why is there a difference between the number of synapses that a child has and the number that an adult has?

HT

5 Number the following statements **1–4** to put them into the correct order.

    a) Neurotransmitters bind with receptors on motor neuron ☐

    b) Electrical signal moves through sensory neuron ☐

    c) Electrical signal sent through motor neuron ☐

    d) Chemicals released into synapse ☐

Brain and Mind

1 a) Explain what is meant by a reflex action.

　

b) i) Paul accidentally put his hand onto the hot plate of an oven. As the plate was burning his hand, he automatically pulled his hand away very quickly. Correctly label what happens at A–D to show how Paul's body responded to the hot plate.

A: ....

B: ....

C: ....

D: ....

　ii) Describe the nervous pathways used in Paul's reflex response.

　

2 Explain how simple reflex actions can help animals to survive.

　

3 a) Explain two simple reflex actions that newborn babies show.

　i) ....

　ii) ....

b) What could it indicate if a newborn baby fails to show one or more of these reflexes?

Brain and Mind

4 Using the diagrams below to help you, explain how the eye can adjust to a) dim light and b) bright light.

a)

b)

---

5 a) What is the name given to the process whereby a reflex can be learned in response to a given stimulus?

....

b) What are the two component parts of a conditioned reflex action?

   i) ....

   ii) ....

c) Who discovered the principle of a conditioned reflex action?

....

d) Add a description for each step of the process of training a dog to salivate when a bell is rung.

   i) ....

Brain and Mind

ii)

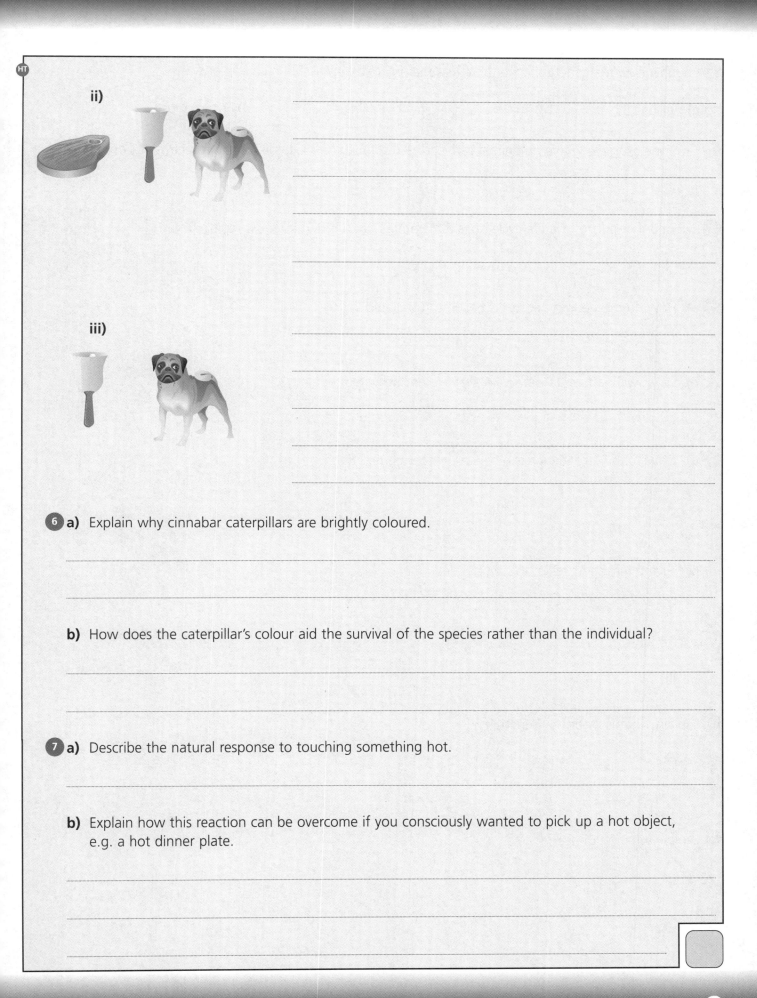

iii)

6 a) Explain why cinnabar caterpillars are brightly coloured.

b) How does the caterpillar's colour aid the survival of the species rather than the individual?

7 a) Describe the natural response to touching something hot.

b) Explain how this reaction can be overcome if you consciously wanted to pick up a hot object, e.g. a hot dinner plate.

Brain and Mind

1 Roughly how many neurons are there in a mammal's brain? Tick the correct answer.

　a) Billions ☐　　b) Trillions ☐　　c) Millions ☐　　d) Thousands ☐

2 Give one example where an animal can learn a response from experience to protect itself from harm.

3 During what part of the life cycle does a mammal's brain grow the most rapidly?

4 a) How do the neuron pathways become stimulated?

　b) What will happen to pathways that are not activated regularly?

5 a) Explain how experience can be learnt through repetition.

　b) Give three examples of this type of learning.

　　i)

　　ii)

　　iii)

6 Explain what is meant by **plasticity**.

7 Explain what a PET scan shows.

Brain and Mind

1 a) Feral children are children that have become isolated from society. Give two examples of how this can happen.

   i) ....

   ii) ....

   b) Genie was a girl in California, USA, who was kept strapped to a potty-chair for 13 years. When discovered at the age of 13 she had suffered severe social and sensory deprivation.

   Suggest how this may have affected Genie's ability to talk.

   ....

   ....

2 a) Give two examples of developmental milestones that a 3-month-old baby should show.

   i) ....

   ii) ....

   b) Give two examples of developmental milestones that a 12-month-old baby should show.

   i) ....

   ii) ....

   c) What might it mean if babies are unable to show the developmental milestones given in your answers to **a)** and **b)** above.

   ....

3 a) Animals are able to adapt to new situations. Give two examples of situations that dogs can be trained for.

   i) ....

   ii) ....

   b) Marine mammals, such as dolphins and whales, can be trained in captivity. Give two examples of what these mammals can be trained to do.

   i) ....

   ii) ....

Brain and Mind

1 The cerebral cortex is the part of our brain concerned with four things. What are they?

a) _____

b) _____

c) _____

d) _____

2 Scientists have used a variety of methods to map the different regions of the cerebral cortex. Explain what the physiological technique is.

_____

_____

_____

3 Name two electronic techniques used for mapping the brain activity and briefly explain how they work.

a) _____

_____

_____

b) _____

_____

_____

4 Using the words below, complete the following sentences.

Memory is the ability to _____ and _____ information. Verbal memory can be divided into _____ memory and _____ memory. Short-term memory is capable of storing a limited amount of _____ for roughly 15–30 seconds. Long-term memory can store a seemingly _____ amount of information indefinitely.

short-term   **long-term**   **store**   **retrieve**   **information**   **unlimited**

5 a) How many pieces of information can be stored in the human brain in the short term?

_____

Brain and Mind

b) How can this amount of information be increased?

c) Using your answer to **b)**, arrange the following numbers in a pattern that will make them easier to remember.

   i) 026485760947   **ii)** 623609580905114

6 a) What effect can drugs have on nerve impulses to the brain?

b) Explain what effect **i)** alcohol, and **ii)** caffeine, has on nerve impulses.

   i)

   ii)

7 What three things are more likely to make information easier to remember? *(HT)*

   a)

   b)

   c)

8 Drugs can affect how the nervous system works.

Describe how the drug Ecstasy (MDMA) affects the synapses in the brain.

9 What is a long-term consequence of taking Ecstasy?

Chemical Synthesis

1) Chemical synthesis deals with how raw materials are made into different products. Name five products that are made in the chemical industry in the UK.

a) ....

b) ....

c) ....

d) ....

e) ....

2) a) What name do we give to a chemical that is produced on a large scale?

....

b) Give two examples of large-scale chemicals.

i) .... ii) ....

3) a) On what scale are fine chemicals produced?

....

b) Give two examples of fine chemicals.

i) .... ii) ....

c) Why is it so important to learn about the raw materials involved in producing chemicals?

....

....

4) a) What is the pH scale?

....

....

b) Briefly describe what you understand by **i)** acid, and **ii)** alkali.

i) ....

ii) ....

....

Chemical Synthesis

5 a) For the following colours in the pH scale, say how acidic, alkaline or neutral a substance would be.

  i) Green .... **ii)** Deep red ....

  iii) Deep purple .... **iv)** Light yellow ....

  v) Light green ....

b) Give an example of a substance that is **i)** very acidic, **ii)** neutral, and **iii)** very alkaline.

  i) .... **ii)** ....

  iii) ....

c) How is the pH of a substance measured?

....

6 Five compounds are listed below as formulae: **i)** write down the name of each compound, and **ii)** say whether each one is an acid or an alkali.

a) NaOH

  i) .... **ii)** ....

b) H_2SO_4

  i) .... **ii)** ....

c) $Ca(OH)_2$

  i) .... **ii)** ....

d) HCl

  i) .... **ii)** ....

e) KOH

  i) .... **ii)** ....

7 What is produced when **a)** acidic compounds, and **b)** alkali compounds dissolve in water?

a) ....

b) ....

Chemical Synthesis

1 a) Briefly describe what you understand by the term **neutralisation**.

b) What is the pH of the solution produced in a neutralisation reaction?

c) Write a word equation to show what happens in general terms during neutralisation.

d) Write a symbol equation for what happens, in terms of ions, during neutralisation.

2 a) What are the two main factors that influence what kind of salt is produced during neutralisation?

   i)

   ii)

b) What kind of salts are produced by…

   i) hydrochloric acid?

   ii) sulfuric acid?

   iii) nitric acid?

3 Complete the following word and formulaic equations to show which salts are being produced during neutralisation reactions.

   a) Sulfuric acid + Copper oxide $\longrightarrow$ .... + Water

   b) $HCl_{(aq)} + NaOH_{(aq)} \longrightarrow$ .... $+ H_2O_{(l)}$

   c) Nitric acid + Potassium hydroxide $\longrightarrow$ .... + Water

   d) $2HNO_{3(aq)} + CaCO_{3(aq)} \longrightarrow$ .... $+ H_2O_{(l)}$

Chemical Synthesis

1 a) Write down the names and formulae for three Group 1 salts.

i) _____

ii) _____

iii) _____

b) For the three salts listed above, work out the charges on both ions.

i) _____

ii) _____

iii) _____

2 a) Write down the names and formulae for three Group 2 salts.

i) _____

ii) _____

iii) _____

b) For the three salts listed above, work out the charges on both ions.

i) _____

ii) _____

iii) _____

3 List the names of the four common gases and their formulae.

a) _____ b) _____

c) _____ d) _____

4 a) When chemical synthesis takes place, what tends to happen to the product if more reactants are used?

_____

b) Write the word equation for the calculation of percentage yield.

_____

Chemical Synthesis

5 Complete the list below to show the seven key stages to the chemical synthesis of an inorganic compound.

  i) Establish the reaction or series of reactions.

  ii) Carry out a _____ _____ .

  iii) Carry out the reaction under suitable conditions, e.g. _____ , concentration and the presence of a catalyst.

  iv) Separate the _____ from the reaction mixture.

  v) _____ the product to make sure it is not contaminated by products or reactants.

  vi) Measure the _____ .

  vii) Check the _____ .

6 Using the stages listed in question **5** above, answer the following questions.

  a) Imagine that in Stage 1 you have decided to make zinc chloride by mixing zinc with hydrochloric acid. Write the word equation for this reaction.

  b) Describe briefly what safety precautions you would take before carrying out this experiment.

  c) Write down one way that you could remove the excess zinc that has not reacted.

  d) If the actual yield of the zinc chloride is 5g and the theoretical yield is 10g, calculate the percentage yield.

Chemical Synthesis

1 List three things that you need to understand in order to work out how much starting material (or reactant) is needed to make a known amount of product.

   a) _____

   b) _____

   c) _____

2 a) Using the Periodic Table on **p.96** to help, find out the relative atomic mass of the following elements:

   i) Aluminium _____   ii) Chlorine _____

   iii) Nitrogen _____   iv) Germanium _____

   v) Calcium _____

b) What do your answers for **a)** also represent for each element?

   _____

3 a) i) Briefly describe what the relative formula mass of a compound is.

   _____

   ii) What is the symbol for relative atomic mass?

   _____

b) What two things do we need to know in order to calculate the relative formula mass of a compound?

   i) _____

   ii) _____

c) Using the Periodic Table on **p.96** to help, calculate the relative formula mass of the following compounds:

   i) Copper sulfate _____

   ii) Sulfuric acid _____

   iii) Ammonia _____

Chemical Synthesis

1) Calcium carbonate and hydrochloric acid react together to produce calcium chloride, carbon dioxide and water. Below is the balanced symbol equation for this reaction.

$$CaCO_{3(s)} + 2HCl_{(aq)} \longrightarrow CaCl_{2(aq)} + CO_{2(g)} + H_2O_{(l)}$$

a) Work out the M_r for each of the reactants and products shown in the equation and write them below.

　　i) $CaCO_3$ _____　　ii) $2HCl$ _____　　iii) $CaCl_2$ _____

　　iv) CO_2 _____　　v) H_2O _____

b) What is the total mass of all the reactants in the equation?

c) What is the total mass of all the products in the equation?

d) Would you have expected the masses in parts **b)** and **c)** to be the same? Explain your answer.

e) What mass of calcium chloride can be produced from 2g of calcium carbonate?

2) Referring to the equation in question **1** above, how much calcium carbonate is needed to produce 1kg (1000g) of calcium chloride?

Chemical Synthesis

1 a) Briefly describe how titrations can be used to calculate the purity of an acid.

_____

_____

b) Complete the six definitions below which describe the key steps in the titration process.

i) Fill a _____ with the _____, e.g. sodium hydroxide.

ii) Accurately weigh out a sample of acid and dissolve it in _____ _____.

iii) _____ a specified proportion of the aqueous _____ and put it into a conical flask.

iv) Add a few drops of phenolphthalein, an _____. It will stay _____. Put the flask on a white tile under the _____.

v) Add _____ from the _____ into the flask.

vi) _____ this procedure until you get two results that are the _____.

2 To calculate the purity of an acid, you need to work in dm³. How do you convert cm³ into dm³?

_____

3 Using your knowledge of the titration process, answer the following questions.

a) Briefly describe how you calculate the concentration of acid you have used in your titration.

_____

_____

_____

b) What is the word formula for calculating the actual mass of acid you have used?

_____

c) What is the word formula for calculating the percentage of purity of the acid?

_____

_____

Chemical Synthesis

1 a) What do particles need to do to cause a chemical reaction?

b) Give **i)** one example of a slow chemical reaction, and **ii)** one example of a fast reaction.

i) .... ii) ....

2 What are the three main ways in which the rate of a chemical reaction can be measured?

a) ....

b) ....

c) ....

3 Use the graph opposite to answer the following questions.

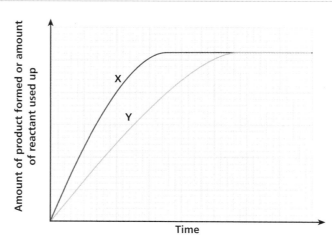

a) Which reaction is faster – X or Y? How can we tell this by looking at the graph?

b) Give three reasons why this reaction might be faster than Y.

i) ....

ii) ....

iii) ....

c) What does the flat line on the graph tell us?

d) What does not change, irrespective of the rate of reaction?

Chemical Synthesis

1 List the four key factors that affect the rate of a chemical reaction.

a) .... b) ....

c) .... d) ....

2 What happens to particles when they are…

a) at a low temperature?

....

....

b) at a high temperature?

....

....

....

3 What happens in a reaction where one or both reactants are…

a) in low concentrations?

....

....

b) in high concentrations?

....

....

4 Complete the table below to show the properties of large and small particles in relation to their surface area.

	Surface Area	Collisions	Reaction Rate
Large Particles			
Small Particles			

5 What is a **catalyst**?

....

....

Chemical Synthesis

6) The decomposition of hydrogen peroxide is one example of a reaction that can involve a catalyst (in this case manganese (IV) oxide).

   a) At what speed does this reaction occur, unless we add the manganese (IV) oxide?

   b) What physical reaction can you see as the oxygen is given off?

HT

7) a) When there is an increase in temperature, the kinetic energy of particles tends to also increase. What does this mean?

   b) How does this impact on the collisions between particles?

   c) What effect does increasing concentration or surface area have on the collision between particles?

8) In terms of the collisions between particles, how does a catalyst work?

9) Why do you only need a small amount of a catalyst in a chemical reaction?

10) List **a)** one safety, **b)** one environmental, and **c)** one economic factor that you would need to consider if you were producing a pharmaceutical product on an industrial scale.

   a)

   b)

   c)

The Wave Model of Radiation

1 Complete the following sentences.

All waves transfer _____ from one place to another without transferring _____.

The _____ is transferred in the direction the wave _____. There are two types of wave: _____ and _____.

2 a) Describe the difference between longitudinal and transverse waves.

_____

_____

_____

_____

b) Give an example of each type of wave.

i) Longitudinal: _____

ii) Transverse: _____

3 Explain what is meant by the frequency of a wave.

_____

_____

4 Use the axis below to sketch a wave. Mark up the amplitude, frequency and wavelength.

5 All electromagnetic waves travel at the same speed in a vacuum but have different frequencies. How does the wavelength depend on the frequency?

_____

_____

The Wave Model of Radiation

6 When a wave passes from one medium to another its speed will often change but its frequency stays the same. If the wave slows down, what effect does this have on the wavelength?

....

....

7 Write down the formula linking wave speed, frequency and wavelength.

....

8 For the following questions, tick the correct answer.

a) A sound wave has a wavelength of 2m and a frequency of 150Hz. What is the wave speed?

i) 0.013m/s ☐   ii) 3m/s ☐   iii) 75m/s ☐   iv) 300m/s ☐   v) 30 000m/s ☐

b) A pebble dropped in a pond creates a wave with a frequency of 3Hz and a wavelength of 6cm. What is the wave speed?

i) 0.18m/s ☐   ii) 1.8m/s ☐   iii) 18m/s ☐   iv) 0.02m/s ☐   v) 2m/s ☐

c) A sound wave travelling in a block of steel has a frequency of 10kHz and a wavelength of 50cm. What is the wave speed?

i) 5m/s ☐   ii) 50m ☐   iii) 500m/s ☐   iv) 5000m/s ☐   v) 50 000m/s ☐

HT

9 Complete the following table:

Wave Speed	Frequency	Wavelength
a)	600kHz	500m
1500m/s	6kHz	b)
300 000 000m/s	c)	500nm (5×10^{-9}m)

10 Radio 1 transmits in the range of frequencies 97–100MHz with the exact value depending on where you live in the country.

Taking 300 000 000m/s as the wave speed of radio waves, what is the range of wavelengths that Radio 1 transmits on?

....

....

The Wave Model of Radiation

1 In which three ways can light, sound and water waves act?

a) .... b) .... c) ....

2 What happens to the speed and direction of a wavelength when a water wave crosses a boundary between one medium and another? Complete the diagram below to help you explain your answer.

3 a) When waves pass through a narrow gap they are diffracted. What does this mean?

b) What happens when a wave passes through a gap much larger than its wavelength?

4 The picture below shows a house in the shadow of a hill. Use ideas about diffraction to explain why the house is able to receive the long-wave radio signals from the transmitter, but light from the transmitter is unable to reach the house.

5 On the diagram below add the normal line and label the angles of incidence and reflection.

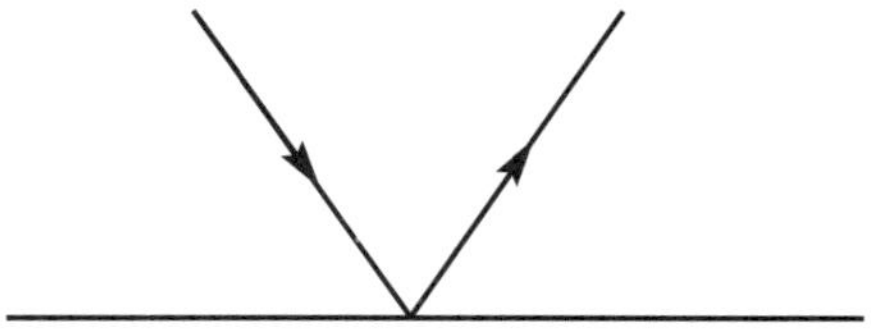

6 Explain what the **i)** incident ray, and **ii)** reflected ray is.

i) ....

ii) ....

The Wave Model of Radiation

1) On the diagrams below, sketch the path of a light ray as it enters and leaves the glass block. Label the normal and the angles of incidence and refraction.

2) Explain why a light wave changes direction when it passes from one medium into another.

....

....

....

3) When light travels from a dense medium to a less dense medium, e.g. glass into air, the angle of refraction can be greater than 90°. What is this called and what happens to the light ray?

....

....

4) Are the following statements **true** or **false**?

a) When waves are in step their amplitudes add up. ....

b) When waves are out of step their amplitudes add up. ....

c) Destructive interference means that the waves explode. ....

d) Constructive interference means that the amplitudes of the waves add up. ....

5) Freak waves can sometimes occur when waves at sea constructively interfere. Why can this be dangerous for ships?

....

....

....

The Wave Model of Radiation

1) What is a photon?

....

2) Number the following wavelengths 1–7 to put them into the correct order, starting with the highest frequency and photon energy first.

a) Microwaves ☐   b) X-rays ☐   c) Radio waves ☐   d) Ultraviolet ☐

e) Gamma rays ☐   f) Visible light ☐   g) Infrared rays ☐

3) What are the three main differences between sound waves and electromagnetic waves?

a) ....

b) ....

c) ....

4) At what speed do electromagnetic waves travel through space?

....

5) The power of a beam of radiation depends on two things. One is the number of photons delivered by the beam of radiation every second. What is the other?

....

6) What two facts support the idea that electromagnetic radiation travel as waves?

a) ....

b) ....

The Wave Model of Radiation

7 a) On the diagram below, show what happens to white light as it passes through the prism.

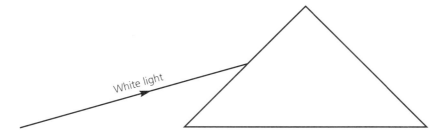

b) Explain your answer to part **a)**.

8 Match the types of radiation to their uses.

Type of Radiation
Radio Waves
Light and Infrared
Microwaves
X-rays

Use
Taking shadow pictures of bones.
Transmitting radio and TV programmes.
Satellite communications. Heating food.
Carrying information on computer networks and telephone cables.

9 Explain how the properties of microwaves make them suitable for sending signals through the Earth's atmosphere.

10 Explain how the properties of X-rays make them suitable for their uses.

The Wave Model of Radiation

1 For a wave to carry a signal it must be modulated. Complete the table below with a description and a diagram showing the output wave of the two types of modulation.

Description	Diagram
a)	
Frequency Modulation. The frequency of the output wave changes but the amplitude remains constant.	b)

2 Explain the difference between an analogue and a digital signal. Draw diagrams to help you explain your answer.

3 On the axis below sketch the digital signal represented by 1011001.

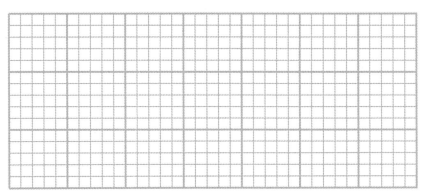

The Wave Model of Radiation

4) On the axis below sketch an analogue wave with a wavelength of 2cm and an amplitude of 1cm.

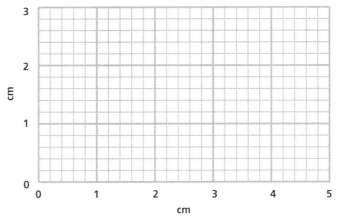

5) When talking about signals we often talk about 'noise'. What do we mean by **signal noise**?

6) The two diagrams below show analogue and digital signals which have been distorted by noise. Explain why digital signals are more tolerant of noise and why this is a benefit.

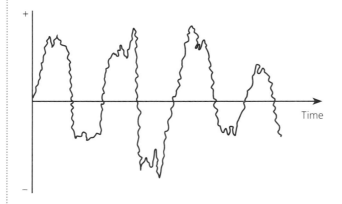
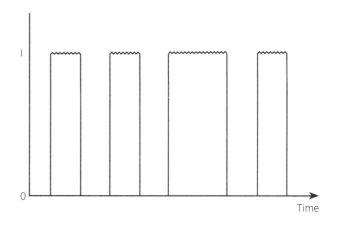

Ideas in Context

The information below is about brain development.

A new study has shown that autism could potentially be caused by delayed neuron development in the first year of a baby's life. Previous studies suggested that it could be due to faster development of the brain.

Autistic people suffer from social and communication problems; they are very attuned to visual imagery, but often have problems understanding language. Post mortem studies have shown that autistic people have significantly fewer nerve cells in the part of the brain that processes emotions, and have poor connections to the part of the brain that interprets language. This would explain the social isolation which is characteristic of the disorder, although it has also been suggested that poor brain connections could be a result of reduced social experience.

Previous studies have shown that the brains of autistic children undergo an unusual and very fast growth spurt in the first year of their lives; this leads to a bigger head size. MRI brain scans have shown that autistic children have brains that are enlarged by about 10%. However, despite having a larger brain, autistic children appear to lack the neuronal development of non-autistic children.

During normal development, the brain grows at a fast pace for the first six months and then at a slower rate until the baby is 18 months old. As the brain slowly grows, the pathways between neurons are stimulated in response to sensory or motor experiences. Every time the experience is repeated after that, the pathway is strengthened. Pathways which are not used regularly are eventually deleted. If, as with autistic children, the brain continues to grow at a very fast pace, the pathways develop so rapidly that experience does not have a chance to determine which ones to keep or destroy.

The new study examined the brain development of children aged between three and four. Normal development was compared to children with autism using a technique which measures the amount of water in brain tissue. In normal development, as the brain develops, water is incorporated into neurons and becomes fixed. However, in autistic brain tissue there was found to be more water that had not become fixed, which suggests a delay in neuronal development.

Scientists have suggested that the delay could be a result of inflammation in the first year of life. Inflammation could affect neuron connections at a critical stage of brain development, leading to learning difficulties as the child develops. There are certain key developmental stages for learning a language. If these stages are missed, then learning a language later in the development process can be more difficult.

Current research has concentrated on finding a gene that could be responsible for rapid, early development, but due to this new information, scientists could now focus their attention onto looking for a gene that produces a susceptibility to inflammation.

Ideas in Context

1 a) What does the new study suggest is the **cause** of autism? Tick the correct answer.

  i) Bigger head size ☐

  ii) Faster development of the brain ☐

  iii) Delayed neuron development ☐

  iv) Smaller brains ☐

b) An MRI scan is a type of electronic technique used to scan the brain. What did MRI scans of autistic children show?

....

c) What is an outward indicator of faster brain growth?

....

d) What two things do autistic people have problems with?

  i) ....

  ii) ....

e) Why does increased brain development at a young age mean that experiences are not retained?

....

....

....

HT f) Poor brain connections could also be a result of reduced social experiences. Suggest what this means.

....

g) If autistic children do not learn language skills at the correct time, why might it be harder for them later in life?

....

Ideas in Context

The information below is about using electromagnetic radiation and chemical analysis to detect explosives.

Following the recent foiling of an alleged terrorist plot to blow up transatlantic passenger flights using the liquid explosive triacetone triperoxide (TATP), attention is being focused on new detection and scanning technologies.

The fear is that explosives could be disguised in everyday objects such as fizzy-drink bottles. However, explosives experts say that extra security measures were put in place as an extra precaution, not because liquid explosives are difficult to detect. In fact, liquid explosives could be easier to detect as they have to be kept in a container, whereas solid explosives come in a variety of shapes and sizes and have no defined form.

Chemical Analysis

Although X-ray machines are used to search luggage, explosive equipment such as detonators can be hidden inside electronic equipment, so chemical analysis can be used to detect them. A swab can be taken from a bag and placed into a machine that heats up the sample and performs a spectrographic analysis of the vapours. The machine searches for traces of nitrogen, as this is found in the majority of explosives.

Experts say that although it would not be possible to perform a careful chemical analysis on every bottle of liquid to be carried onto the plane, it might be possible to ban any non water-based liquids and have a simple test to pick these out using universal indicator paper.

Electronic Techniques

Experts say improved airport scanning that detects explosives remains a top priority. The most commonly used X-ray scanning devices are used to detect suspicious shapes, such as the pattern of wires likely to be found in a bomb. But there may be the need for even more sophisticated scanning techniques. Some new machines can detect specific compounds by measuring reflected X-ray photons. They can reveal materials made up of elements which have a low atomic number (as explosives are) such as hydrogen and nitrogen.

Another more sophisticated detection method is scanning with terahertz waves, which lie between microwaves and infrared on the electromagnetic spectrum. At the moment these scanners are very large and their use in airports would be impractical, but portable scanners are being developed. These scanners could measure the way objects absorb and reflect terahertz waves, as they pass straight through plastic, fabric, wood and stone but can be used to spot other compounds, including certain drugs, metals and explosives.

Ideas in Context

1 a) What do X-ray scanners do?

b) How do X-ray scanners work? Place a tick beside the correct answer.

   i) X-rays are absorbed by dense materials. ☐

   ii) X-rays are emitted by dense materials. ☐

   iii) X-rays are reflected by dense materials. ☐

c) Would a liquid explosive be harder to detect than a solid explosive by an X-ray machine? Explain your answer.

2 What could chemical analysis be used for?

3 a) Name two elements commonly used in explosives.

   i)

   ii)

b) What do these elements have in common?

4 What is a photon?

5 If terahertz radiation is between infrared and microwaves in the electromagnetic spectrum, does this have a low or high frequency?

Glossary

1 Write the following definitions in the spaces provided below.

a) **4 letters**

   A compound with a pH lower than 7 _____.

b) **6 letters**

   i) A compound with a pH higher than 7 _____.

   ii) An electric circuit where there is one path for the current to take _____.

   iii) An automatic, involuntary reaction _____.

c) **7 letters**

   i) A signal which has an on / off state _____.

   ii) Cell division that forms daughter cells with the same number of chromosomes as the parent cell _____.

   iii) The diffusion of water from a high concentration to a low concentration _____.

d) **8 letters**

   i) Produces a response to a stimulus _____.

   ii) The speed and direction of an object _____.

e) **9 letters**

   i) The maximum disturbance caused by a wave _____.

   ii) The total force acting on an object _____.

f) **11 letters**

   i) A condition where the body temperature drops too low _____.

   ii) Adapted for a particular purpose _____.

   iii) An electric current which changes direction _____.

g) **13 letters**

   The fusion of male and female nuclei _____.

Glossary

2 Complete this wordsearch using all your answers from question **1** on p.91

P	A	A	L	T	E	R	N	A	T	I	N	G	A	L	J
A	B	O	C	R	X	Q	B	D	V	E	S	I	U	E	P
K	W	P	H	H	S	U	A	N	E	L	I	E	D	N	I
A	I	G	M	F	W	R	C	K	L	L	S	U	O	T	H
M	Q	A	L	K	A	L	I	Q	O	S	O	Q	B	P	F
P	D	R	I	Y	R	M	D	V	C	N	T	C	E	E	M
L	A	O	S	F	D	B	O	D	I	A	I	J	R	R	T
I	I	S	S	E	P	I	U	H	T	Z	M	T	E	S	O
T	M	M	V	D	R	X	B	F	Y	B	I	S	D	T	X
U	R	O	R	T	Y	I	K	D	F	L	U	A	I	R	M
D	E	S	E	H	I	M	E	I	I	L	S	O	G	G	D
E	H	I	F	E	B	G	L	S	T	Z	R	B	I	F	V
E	T	S	L	N	L	D	A	A	D	P	Y	N	T	J	J
G	O	P	E	B	F	T	N	T	Q	K	Q	J	A	X	I
A	P	T	X	S	I	T	S	H	G	R	T	M	L	B	S
I	Y	A	L	O	T	Q	G	S	J	L	Y	B	H	R	P
N	H	E	N	K	P	F	W	V	B	R	H	M	P	D	G
P	D	T	O	Q	R	O	T	C	E	F	F	E	G	U	X
K	O	D	E	S	I	L	A	I	C	E	P	S	C	M	Z
V	B	B	Q	V	N	Y	F	N	P	S	A	I	U	J	K

Notes

Notes

Notes

Periodic Table

Key

1	
H	
hydrogen	
1	

- Relative atomic mass
- Atomic symbol
- Name
- Atomic (proton) number

1	2												3	4	5	6	7	8 or 0
						1 **H** hydrogen 1												4 **He** helium 2
7 **Li** lithium 3	9 **Be** beryllium 4												11 **B** boron 5	12 **C** carbon 6	14 **N** nitrogen 7	16 **O** oxygen 8	19 **F** fluorine 9	20 **Ne** neon 10
23 **Na** sodium 11	24 **Mg** magnesium 12												27 **Al** aluminium 13	28 **Si** silicon 14	31 **P** phosphorus 15	32 **S** sulfur 16	35.5 **Cl** chlorine 17	40 **Ar** argon 18
39 **K** potassium 19	40 **Ca** calcium 20	45 **Sc** scandium 21	48 **Ti** titanium 22	51 **V** vanadium 23	52 **Cr** chromium 24	55 **Mn** manganese 25	56 **Fe** iron 26	59 **Co** cobalt 27	59 **Ni** nickel 28	63.5 **Cu** copper 29	65 **Zn** zinc 30		70 **Ga** gallium 31	73 **Ge** germanium 32	75 **As** arsenic 33	79 **Se** selenium 34	80 **Br** bromine 35	84 **Kr** krypton 36
85 **Rb** rubidium 37	88 **Sr** strontium 38	89 **Y** yttrium 39	91 **Zr** zirconium 40	93 **Nb** niobium 41	96 **Mo** molybdenum 42	98 **Tc** technetium 43	101 **Ru** ruthenium 44	103 **Rh** rhodium 45	106 **Pd** palladium 46	108 **Ag** silver 47	112 **Cd** cadmium 48		115 **In** indium 49	119 **Sn** tin 50	122 **Sb** antimony 51	128 **Te** tellurium 52	127 **I** iodine 53	131 **Xe** xenon 54
133 **Cs** caesium 55	137 **Ba** barium 56	139 **La*** lanthanum 57	178 **Hf** hafnium 72	181 **Ta** tantalum 73	184 **W** tungsten 74	186 **Re** rhenium 75	190 **Os** osmium 76	192 **Ir** iridium 77	195 **Pt** platinum 78	197 **Au** gold 79	201 **Hg** mercury 80		204 **Tl** thallium 81	207 **Pb** lead 82	209 **Bi** bismuth 83	210 **Po** polonium 84	210 **At** astatine 85	222 **Rn** radon 86
223 **Fr** francium 87	226 **Ra** radium 88	227 **Ac*** actinium 89	261 **Rf** rutherfordium 104	262 **Db** dubnium 105	266 **Sg** seaborgium 106	264 **Bh** bohrium 107	277 **Hs** hassium 108	268 **Mt** meitnerium 109	271 **Ds** darmstadtium 110	272 **Rg** roentgenium 111								

*The Lanthanides (atomic numbers 58-71) and the Actinides (atomic numbers 90-103) have been omitted. Cu and Cl have not been rounded to the nearest whole number.

→ The lines of elements going across are called periods.

→ The columns of elements going down are called groups.